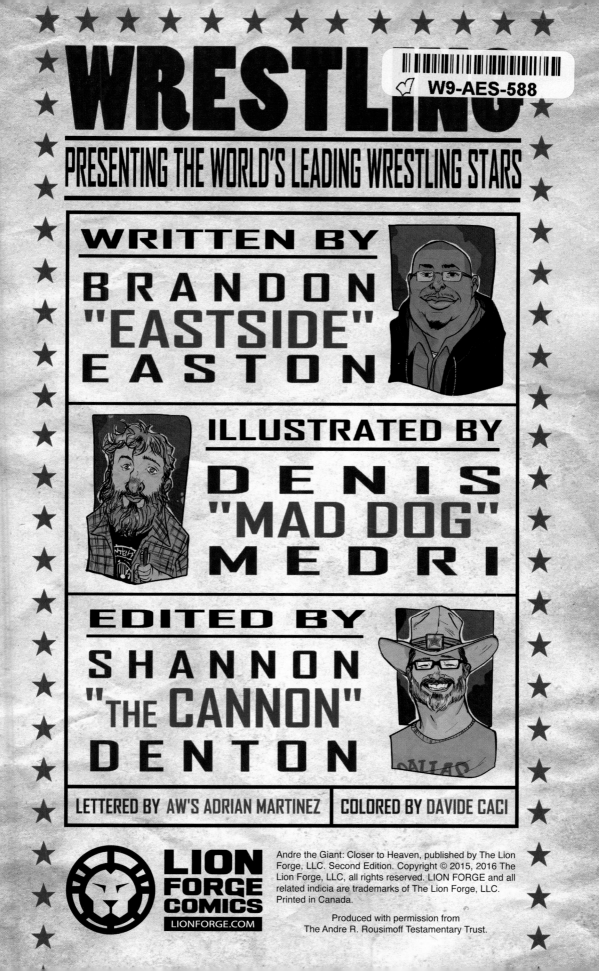

WRESTLING

PRESENTING THE WORLD'S LEADING WRESTLING STARS

WRITTEN BY

BRANDON "EASTSIDE" EASTON

ILLUSTRATED BY

DENIS "MAD DOG" MEDRI

EDITED BY

SHANNON "THE CANNON" DENTON

LETTERED BY AW'S ADRIAN MARTINEZ | COLORED BY DAVIDE CACI

LION FORGE COMICS
LIONFORGE.COM

Andre the Giant: Closer to Heaven, published by The Lion Forge, LLC. Second Edition. Copyright © 2015, 2016 The Lion Forge, LLC, all rights reserved. LION FORGE and all related indicia are trademarks of The Lion Forge, LLC. Printed in Canada.

Produced with permission from The Andre R. Rousimoff Testamentary Trust.

FOREWORD

From as early as I can remember, I knew my father was a celebrity. Although he wasn't in my life, I could see him whenever I wanted. On TV, in magazines, even in movies - Andre the Giant's public persona seemed to be everywhere. But I barely knew the man that Andre Roussimoff was when there were no cameras, fans or crowds around.

One of my earliest memories of my father was a surprise visit he made to my daycare. I must've been about four years old. My teacher must've had an interesting sight, a huge mountain of a man in a room full of tiny children. But his visits with me would be scarce, since his profession had always consumed his life. He didn't belong to me or even my mother, though they were together for seven years - despite rumors to the contrary. He belonged to the media and to professional wrestling, which kept him on the road nonstop. And sadly, his illness and personal struggles with alcohol made it even more difficult for him to be the father he may have wanted to be.

But unlike most kids who grow up without a father, I could connect with my dad in other ways. My mother brought me to see The Princess Bride. When the character of Fezzik appeared on screen I yelled out "That's my dad!" in the crowded theater. I was so excited, my mother had to pop her hand over my mouth.

Soon after that I went to see him at one of his wrestling matches. I sat on his lap, and this giant man who fought other large men for a living was trying his hardest to find common ground with an 8-year-old girl. He wanted to take an interest in my life, things like my gymnastics lessons or the music that I liked. And then he disappeared to go on the road again. Being Andre the Giant's daughter was a fact I soon learned to keep to myself. If I told people they would accuse me of lying. If they believed me, they would try to use me as a connection to him.

The last time I spoke to my father was the Christmas before he died. During the phone call I thanked him for my gift. Once again, he tried to connect with me. Making small talk about whether it would snow for the holidays - we lived in Washington where it never did. He always asked about my hobbies and interests, things a dad should know. No matter how violent he was in the ring, I'll forever remember him as a sweet man who always had a smile for me. But as the book details, I was able to write him a letter expressing my frustration at his lack of involvement in my life. It was the only closure I would ever have.

A few months later, we came home to find a message from my father's lawyer on the answering machine with the news that my dad had passed away. He wanted us to know before the media ran the story. I was just 13 years old. Maybe had he lived longer, I might have had a closer relationship with him. Perhaps he would've attended my graduation, or been proud of my successes. I'll never get to really know who he really was as a person, as opposed to the identity that the media and his employers manufactured for him.

What struck me when reading this graphic novel was the honest way it portrayed my father - not as just the wrestler or actor, but as the human being. He made mistakes and had many struggles in his life. I hope this book helps people realize that Andre the Giant was just a man who did the best he could do. Brandon Easton, the author, also portrayed my relationship with my father in one of the most truthful ways I've seen.

My mother and I were at the center of many rumors and outright lies. It was refreshing to see the truth about us instead of a storyline conceived to sell more tickets. Since my mother had a difficult time talking about my father, many parts of his private life are still a mystery to me. I hope when people read this graphic novel, they will get answers not only to who Andre the Giant was as an entertainer, but who Andre Roussimoff was as a person.

-Robin Christensen Roussimoff,
daughter of Andre "The Giant" Roussimoff

EVEN AT THAT YOUNG AGE, THERE WAS A PART OF ME THAT WAS MONSTROUS.

NOT IN TEMPERAMENT, BUT IN HOW OTHERS SAW ME.

IN THAT RING MY SIZE WOULD BE A VIRTUE...

I'D NEVER CONSIDERED MYSELF AS ANYTHING OTHER THAN A FAN OF THE SPORT.

THAT WAS ABOUT TO CHANGE...

IT WAS TIME TO SAY GOODBYE.

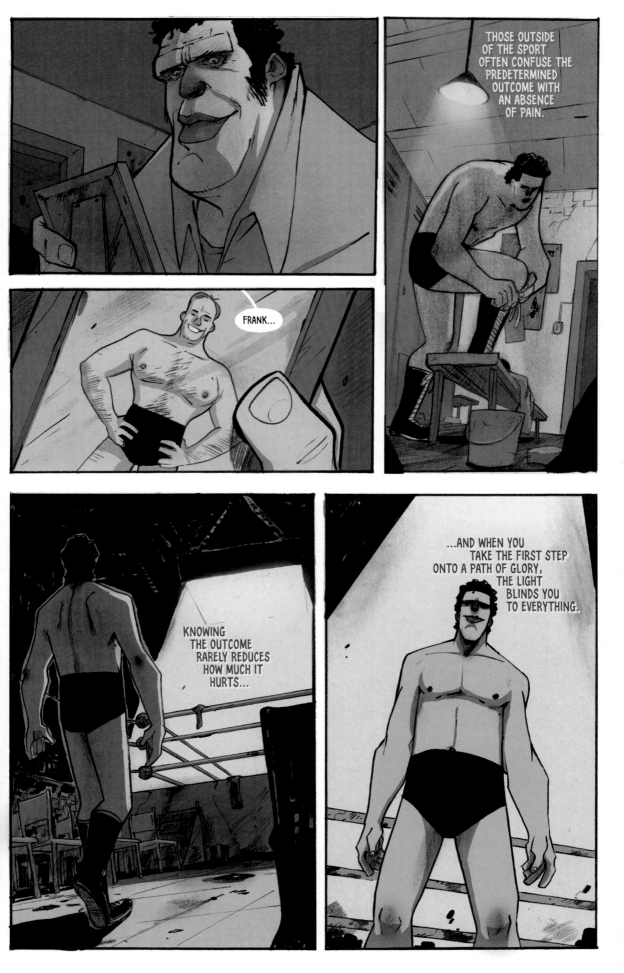

THE TRUE ART OF PROFESSIONAL WRESTLING IS TO SIMULATE VIOLENCE AND TRANSFORM IT INTO THEATER.

THE MOMENT YOU STEP INTO THE RING YOU HAVE TO TRUST THE OTHER GUY TO NOT KILL YOU. NO ONE TRIES TO HARM YOU ON PURPOSE, BUT ALL IT TAKES IS A MISPLACED STEP OR A HARD THRUST, AND A MAN COULD DIE IN AN INSTANT.

THE FIRST TRICKS YOU LEARN ARE "STAND UP" TECHNIQUES. ANYONE CAN TOSS A PUNCH OR A KICK, BUT THE AUDIENCE HAS TO BUY THE MUTUAL AGGRESSION OF THE OPPONENTS. THE COLLAR-AND-ELBOW TIE-UP IS THE FIRST MOVE YOU LEARN. THEY MADE ME REPEAT THIS HUNDREDS OF TIMES. AFTER AN HOUR, I COULDN'T FEEL MY UPPER BODY.

LEARNING HOW TO FALL IS THE KEY TO THE SUSPENSION OF DISBELIEF IN THE RING. A WRESTLER HAS TO UNLEARN SELF-PRESERVATION.

TUCK YOUR CHIN INTO YOUR CHEST, SPREAD YOUR ARMS AND SHOULDERS AND FALL ONTO THE CENTER OF YOUR BACK.

WHEN YOU HIT THE MAT, THE NOISE WILL ECHO ACROSS THE ARENA. IT SOUNDS WORSE THAN IT IS. BUT IT'S GONNA STING NO MATTER WHAT!

WHAP

SORRY.

OVER THE NEXT THREE YEARS, FRANK TAUGHT ME HOW TO "WORK THE CROWD."

TO GET THE DESIRED RESPONSE WITH BODY LANGUAGE AND THE RIGHT PHRASES.

"NEVER GIVE THEM EVERYTHING" WAS FRANK'S MANTRA. HOLD BACK JUST ENOUGH, AND THEY'LL PAY ANYTHING TO SEE YOU GIVE THEM MORE THE NEXT TIME.

HE WAS RIGHT.

BOY, WAS HE RIGHT.

THE PART FRANK NEVER TALKED ABOUT WAS MODERATION. WITH SUCCESS EVERYTHING COMES EASIER, ESPECIALLY VICES. A MAN LEAVING ADOLESCENCE OFTEN CONFUSES EXCESS WITH FREEDOM. PART OF ME WONDERED HOW MANY MEN LEARNED THAT LESSON THE HARD WAY.

THERE WERE THINGS I WAS PREPARED FOR...

AND A FEW NEW SITUATIONS THAT WERE WELCOME DISTRACTIONS.

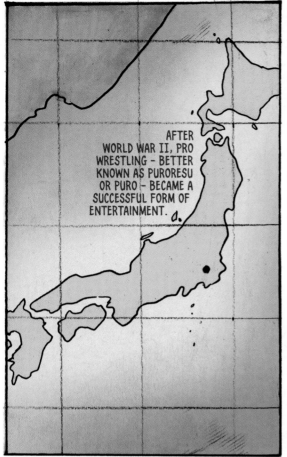

AFTER WORLD WAR II, PRO WRESTLING – BETTER KNOWN AS PURORESU OR PURO – BECAME A SUCCESSFUL FORM OF ENTERTAINMENT.

RIKIDOZAN CAME OF PROMINENCE DURING A TIME WHEN THE JAPANESE NATIONAL SPIRIT WAS DAMAGED AFTER THE DEVASTATION OF HIROSHIMA AND NAGASAKI. HE APPEALED TO THE DESIRES OF THE JAPANESE FANS WHO DESPERATELY WANTED TO SEE A PROUD NATIONAL HERO "STAND UP" TO THE AMERICANS.

RIKIDOZAN AND HIS PEERS DEVELOPED A STYLE OF WRESTLING THAT EMPHASIZED THE SKILL OF THE OPPONENTS INSTEAD OF PURELY THEATRICAL STORYTELLING.

MATCHES ARE TREATED AS LEGITIMATE FIGHTS WITH FULL-CONTACT MARTIAL ARTS BLOWS AND A PACE THAT REQUIRES ALMOST SUPERHUMAN LEVELS OF ENDURANCE.

FRANK BOOKED ME IN THE NUMBER ONE FEDERATION IN JAPAN – *INTERNATIONAL WRESTLING ENTERPRISE* – FOR A TOUR.

THE OWNER, ISAO YOSHIHARA, WAS CERTAIN I WOULD MAKE AN IMPACT ON THE SCENE.

HE HAD NO IDEA HOW BIG.

MY LEGEND WAS GROWING. THE DEMAND TO SEE ME WAS STRONG ACROSS THE GLOBE.

GRAND PRIX CATAPULTED MY CAREER IN WAYS I DIDN'T IMAGINE. WHILE I WAS ALREADY A STAR, I DIDN'T HAVE A *CHARACTER*. I PAID CLOSE ATTENTION TO MY FREQUENT TAG PARTNER ÉDOUARD CARPENTIER. I WATCHED HOW HE BECAME SOMEONE DIFFERENT IN THE RING.

PARTICULARLY IN THE FRENCH-SPEAKING PORTION OF NORTH AMERICA.

MONTREAL, QUEBEC... I'D BEEN BOOKED FOR GRAND PRIX WRESTLING AS THE "EIGHTH WONDER OF THE WORLD."

I LIKED THE SOUND OF THAT.

I HAD TO BECOME HEROIC. MORE THAN JUST A MONSTER... IN GRAND PRIX, THEY CALLED ME "JEAN FERRE".

A CRIME-FIGHTING CRUSADER ON THE SCENE TO STOP THE FORCES OF EVIL FROM PROSPERING IN THE MONTREAL TERRITORY.

TH OK!!!

ONE OF MY BIGGEST RIVALS WAS "KILLER" KOWALSKI. HE WAS ONE OF THE NICEST GUYS IN THE WORLD WHEN OUT OF CHARACTER...

...BUT IN THE RING, HE WAS THE WORST VILLAIN YOU EVER SAW. HE ONCE RIPPED YUKON ERIC'S EAR OFF IN A MATCH. OF COURSE THE GUY'S EAR WAS CAULIFLOWERED AND USELESS, BUT THE FANS DIDN'T KNOW THAT.

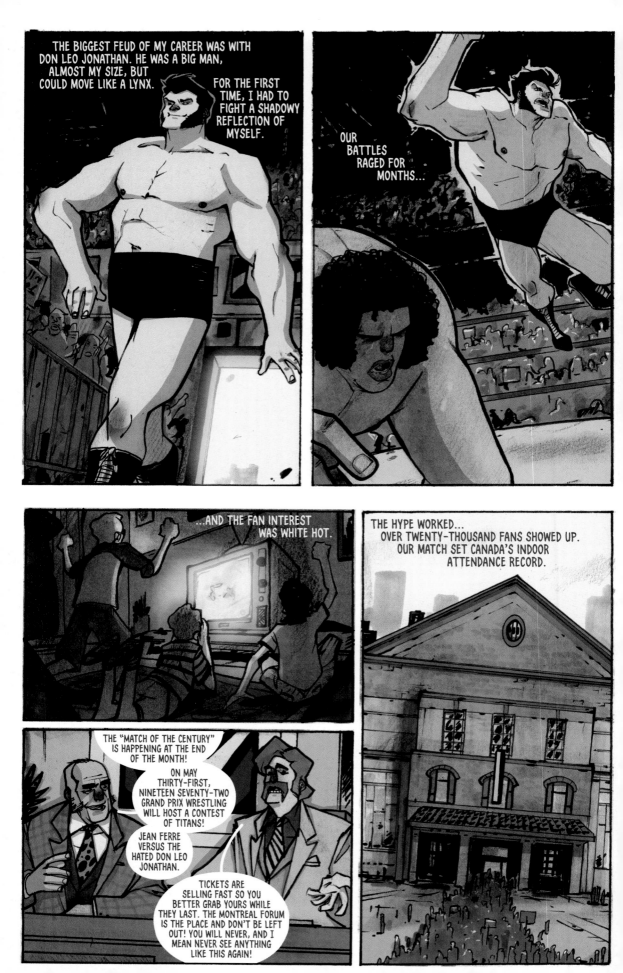

AFTER THAT MATCH, MY LEGEND BECAME AS BIG AS CANADA ITSELF... BUT THERE WAS A HIDDEN COST OF BEING A SUPERHERO.

A HERO IS ONLY VALID IF THEY HAVE AN ENEMY OF EQUAL OR GREATER POWER.

I'D WRESTLED IN EVERY KIND OF MATCH THAT SHOWCASED MY SIZE AND STRENGTH - TWO-ON-ONE MATCHES, THREE-ON-ONE MATCHES LUMBERJACK MATCHES, BATTLE ROYALS... YOU NAME IT, THE FANS SAW IT.

I RAN OUT OF VILLAINS. IN THE MONTREAL TERRITORY, FANS GREW TIRED OF WATCHING ME BEAT UP ON THE SAME GUYS OVER AND OVER AGAIN.

THE GATE RECEIPTS REVEALED THEIR LACK OF ENTHUSIASM.

AFTER A FEW YEARS OF THIS, WHO COULD BLAME THEM?

FRANK HAD BEEN ACTING STRANGE LATELY, I KNEW SOMETHING WAS UP, BUT I COULDN'T FIGURE OUT WHAT WAS UP HIS SLEEVE.

YOU EVER HEARD OF THE WORLD WIDE WRESTLING FEDERATION?

THEY RUN OUT OF THE NORTHEAST TERRITORY OF THE STATES. I THINK THE PROMOTER IS—

HOW? WHAT MAKES HIM DIFFERENT THAN ANY OTHER PROMOTER?

TWO THINGS: *MONEY* AND EXPOSURE. VINCE IS ONE OF THE FEW GUYS OUT THERE THAT ACTUALLY SPLITS THE GATE RECEIPTS WITH THE BOYS. A LOT OF THEM TALK A GOOD GAME, BUT VINCE REALLY DOES IT.

VINCE MCMAHON. THIS GUY KNOWS THE GAME AND HE CAN GET YOU TO THE NEXT LEVEL.

ALL I'M ASKING IS FOR YOU TO MEET THE GUY. WHAT THE WORST THAT COULD HAPPEN? YOU BECOME A BIGGER STAR?

IN THIS BUSINESS, THAT GOES A LONG WAY. AND WE'RE TALKING NEW YORK CITY MAN...

NEW YORK CITY. YOU COULD MAKE MORE MONEY THERE IN A MONTH THAN YOU COULD GOING AROUND THE WORLD IN A YEAR.

OKAY BOSS... LET'S MEET HIM.

IN EVERYONE'S LIFE, YOU REACH A POINT WHERE THERE IS A FORK IN THE ROAD. THERE'S NO GOING BACK, NO SECOND CHANCE, YOU HAVE TO CHOOSE ONE PATH OR THE OTHER.

LITTLE DID I KNOW AT THE TIME, BUT I STEPPED ON A PATH THAT WOULD MAKE ME THE GREATEST STAR IN PRO WRESTLING HISTORY.

IN THOSE DAYS THE WRESTLING SCENE WAS DIVIDED BY REGIONAL TERRITORIES.

EVERY AREA HAD ITS STARS AND THE SMART PROMOTERS KNEW NOT TO STEP ON THE TOES OF THEIR COLLEAGUES.

I WONDERED IF I WAS TOO BIG FOR THOSE TERRITORIES, IF I WOULD PUSH A PROMOTER TO STEP ON TOES, OR RATHER, CRUSH THEM?

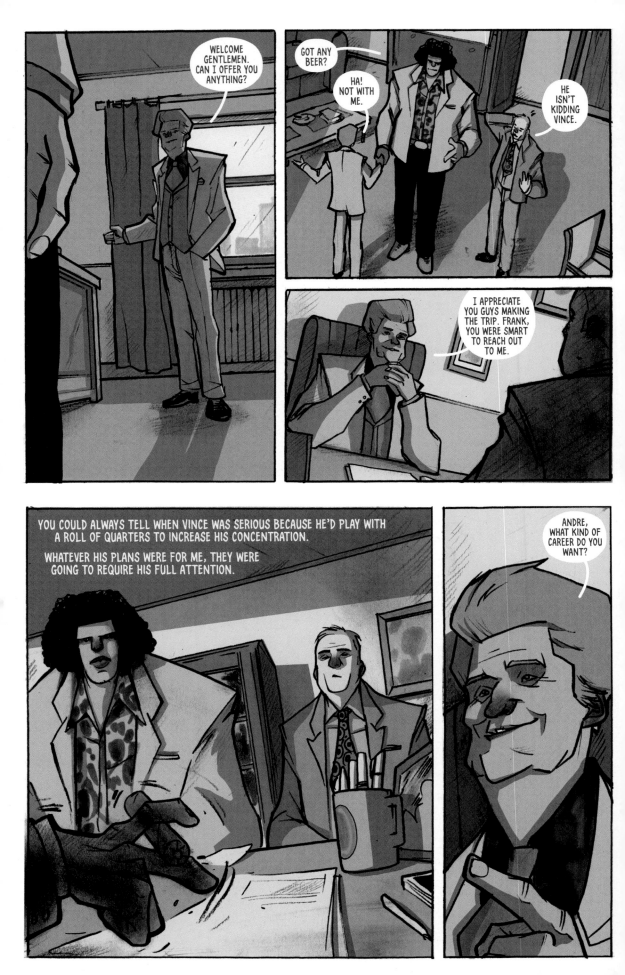

MADISON SQUARE GARDEN.

THE PLACE HAD CHARACTER.

THE SMELL OF BURNT OUT CIGARS FROM GRIZZLED SPORTS REPORTERS...

I LIKE IT HERE.

...MIXED WITH CHEAP COLOGNE, FLAT BEERS, AND STALE POPCORN.

TOPPED WITH AN ODOR THAT I COULDN'T IDENTIFY... EITHER IT WAS WEEK-OLD HOT DOG WATER OR SOMETHING TRULY HORRIBLE LEAKING FROM THE BATHROOMS.

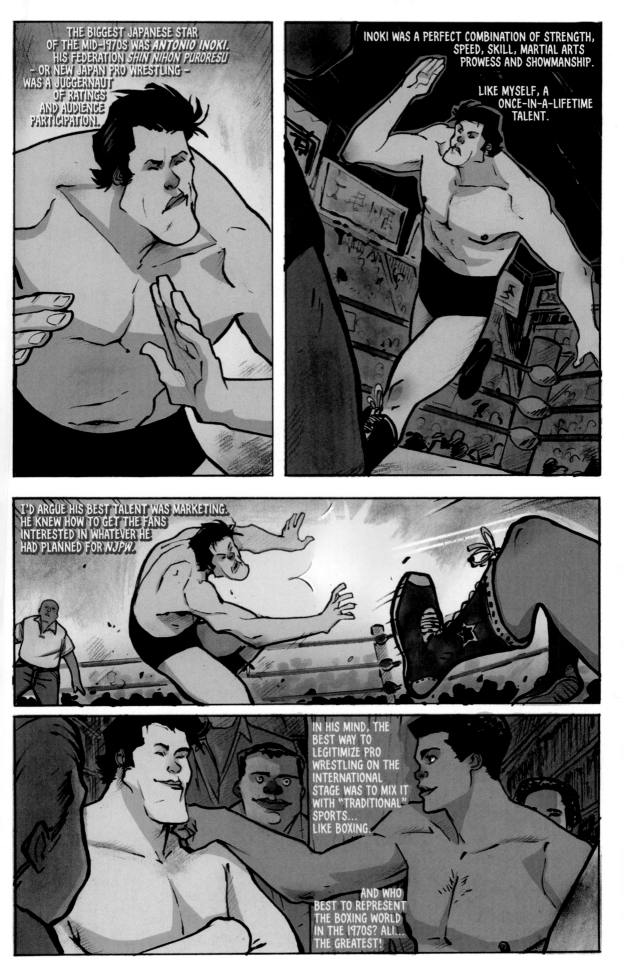

THE BIGGEST JAPANESE STAR OF THE MID-1970S WAS *ANTONIO INOKI.* HIS FEDERATION *SHIN NIHON PURORESU* – OR NEW JAPAN PRO WRESTLING – WAS A JUGGERNAUT OF RATINGS AND AUDIENCE PARTICIPATION.

INOKI WAS A PERFECT COMBINATION OF STRENGTH, SPEED, SKILL, MARTIAL ARTS PROWESS AND SHOWMANSHIP.

LIKE MYSELF, A ONCE-IN-A-LIFETIME TALENT.

I'D ARGUE HIS BEST TALENT WAS MARKETING. HE KNEW HOW TO GET THE FANS INTERESTED IN WHATEVER HE HAD PLANNED FOR *NJPW.*

IN HIS MIND, THE BEST WAY TO LEGITIMIZE PRO WRESTLING ON THE INTERNATIONAL STAGE WAS TO MIX IT WITH "TRADITIONAL" SPORTS... LIKE BOXING.

AND WHO BEST TO REPRESENT THE BOXING WORLD IN THE 1970S? ALI... THE GREATEST!

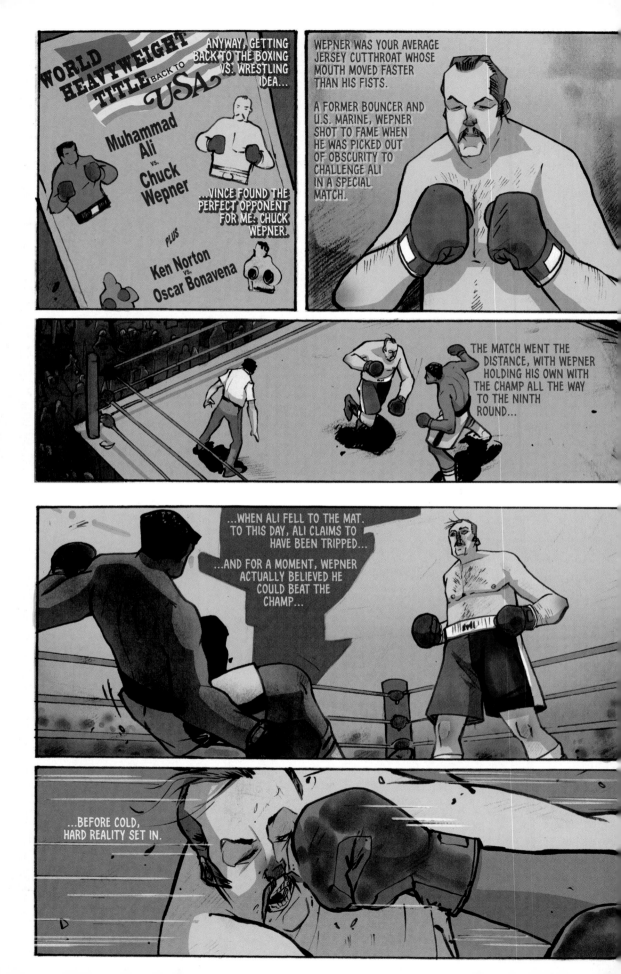

I THINK
HE GOT
THE MESSAGE.

IT WASN'T A MASTERPIECE, BUT IT GOT PEOPLE TALKING.
AND THAT'S WHAT VINCE WANTED ALL ALONG.

AND I'D SETTLED THE "BOXING VS. WRESTLER" DEBATE
ONCE AND FOR ALL. INOKI AND ALI NEVER COULD
FINISH THAT STORY.

SON, THE
WORLD IS
YOURS!

KLASH!

I NEEDED SOMETHING STABLE. THE LIFE OF A WRESTLER IS NOT A CHARMED ONE. YOU LIVE OFF OF THE ADRENALINE... YOU LIVE OFF OF THE ROAR OF THE CROWD... THAT POP WHEN YOU STEP INTO THE ARENA...

...IT ALL LED TO GROUPIES, HUNDREDS OF WILLING LADIES EAGER TO SHOW THEIR APPRECIATION FOR YOU.

I COULD REMEMBER NONE OF THEM.

WELL... THAT'S NOT TRUE... THERE WAS A WOMAN I DATED FOR SEVEN YEARS. IF YOU COULD CALL IT "DATING." HER NAME WAS JEAN.

SHE WRESTLED UNDER THE NAME "TRIXIE COLT" AND WAS AN INTEGRAL PART OF THE SCENE. UNFORTUNATELY, I LET EVERYONE BELIEVE SHE WAS A RING RAT - A COMMON GROUPIE I ENTERTAINED WHENEVER IN THE MOOD.

SHE BECAME PREGNANT AND HAD MY DAUGHTER ROBIN. A MIRACLE REALLY... I WAS TOLD I'D BE STERILE. BECAUSE OF THIS I BELIEVED SHE WAS A LIAR.

Dad... should I call you that? Biologically you're my father, but I've only seen you twice over the last ten years. I'm not writing this letter to blame you for anything. I just want you to know how I feel...

...I understand you believed my mother was lying. You had been told that you couldn't get a woman pregnant. But even after the bloodtest when I was two years old, you still weren't there for me.

In that North Carolina courtroom, it took the weight of the law to get you to finally understand who I was. Years of listening to the wrong people who kept my mother away from you did irreparable damage.

I wished I could have known what it was like to have a dad in my life. I'd take a mailman or carpenter over a global superstar whose shadow hung over our lives.

I know you wanted me to join you on your farm... but I wouldn't come without my mother. I wouldn't go anywhere without mom. I got the impression it hurt you deeply...

...maybe there was a tiny part of me that wanted to hurt you, to make you feel the loss and pain I dealt with every day.

Like I said, I'm not trying to blame you for anything. Nobody was the good guy. We're all responsible for how this turned out.

It's hell... what we need we can't have because it's impossible to reverse time and make better decisions... to have the courage it takes to reach out...

...when we do reach out, all those wrestlers mom thought were her friends have put up a wall around you. They shut us out. Permanently.

I truly hope this letter finds you in good health. Maybe one day we can sit down and just talk. I'd like to know more about you... and I could tell you about my life, my school, my friends... all the little things dads should know.

Until then... best regards.

- Your daughter Robin.

WE'D HAD A SERIES OF BATTLES ACROSS THE NORTHEAST THAT ONLY INTENSIFIED OUR FEUD. THERE HAD BEEN NO CLEAR VICTOR.

THE WAR CULMINATED AT THE "SHOWDOWN AT SHEA."

AUGUST 9 1980

THROUGHOUT MY CAREER, I'D BEEN VERY CAREFUL OF WHO I'D LET GET THE UPPER HAND.

I'D BEEN SLAMMED A FEW TIMES IN JAPAN, BUT THE OLD ADAGE WAS: "IF IT DIDN'T HAPPEN ON TV, IN AMERICA, THEN IT DIDN'T HAPPEN." THE WWF HAD AN INTERESTING WAY OF DEALING WITH PRO WRESTLING HISTORY.

I'D PICKED UP HOGAN TO FINISH HIM OFF WITH A BODY SLAM...

...BUT HIS LEGS POPPED THE REF ON HIS NOGGIN.

WITH THE REF DOWN, HOGAN HAD THE OPPORTUNITY TO BLINDSIDE ME.

WHOOOOOM!

SEVEN YEARS LATER, THE WWF WOULD CLAIM THAT I'D NEVER BEEN SLAMMED BY ANYONE IN MY CAREER.

I GUESS THEY ASSUMED THAT VIDEO TAPES WOULD GO EXTINCT BEFORE 1987... BUT I'LL GET TO THAT LATER.

VINCE HAD A SON ALSO NAMED VINCE. BUT JUNIOR DIDN'T MEET HIS FATHER UNTIL HE WAS A TEENAGER AND THEIR RELATIONSHIP WAS SOMEWHAT STRAINED. JUNIOR WANTED TO BE INVOLVED IN ALL ASPECTS OF THE WRESTLING BIZ, INCLUDING PERFORMING. BUT SENIOR SCOLDED HIM, MAKING SURE HE UNDERSTOOD THE ROLE OF THE PROMOTER IS TO STAY *BEHIND* THE SCENES.

SENIOR SENT JUNIOR TO LEARN THE PROMOTIONAL SIDE OF THE BUSINESS IN SMALLER SECTIONS OF THEIR TERRITORY. JUNIOR TURNED OUT TO BE A FAST LEARNER ON HIS WAS TO BECOMING A GENIUS OF PRO WRESTLING MARKETING AND EXPANSION.

IN JUST A FEW YEARS, JUNIOR OVERSAW THE METEORIC GROWTH OF WWWF TV SYNDICATION ACROSS THE NORTHEAST AND WAS AIMING TO COVER THE ENTIRE NATION WITH THEIR BROADCASTS.

I GOT ALONG FINE WITH JUNIOR. AS LONG AS HIS FATHER WAS THERE TO TEMPER JUNIOR'S AMBITIONS THE COMPANY WAS STABLE AND THE BOYS WERE HAPPY.

IN TIME, SENIOR'S HEALTH WOULD FADE AND JUNIOR WOULD ACQUIRE THE RIGHTS TO CAPITOL WRESTLING CO., LOCK, STOCK AND BARREL. THE WRESTLING BIZ WOULD NEVER BE THE SAME AGAIN.

BUT I'M GETTING AHEAD OF MYSELF...

THE REHAB PROCESS WAS LONG, SLOW AND PAINFUL. THERE WAS NOTHING I COULD DO EXCEPT LET THE HEALING TAKE PLACE.

BY 1983, MY DISEASE FINALLY CAUGHT UP WITH ME. MY BODY COULD NO LONGER GROW, SO THERE WERE CHANGES IN MY PHYSIQUE AND FACE.

IT FELT LIKE I AGED FIVE MONTHS PER WEEK. AT THIS RATE, I'D BE DEAD IN A COUPLE OF YEARS.

I MENTIONED THAT VINCE JUNIOR HAD TAKEN OVER HIS FATHER'S COMPANY. THE DEAL WAS FINALIZED IN '83 AND JUNIOR IMMEDIATELY BEGAN TO CHANGE HOW THINGS WERE DONE.

JUNIOR'S VISION WAS TO TAKE PRO WRESTLING FROM A REGIONAL, INTIMATE ENTERTAINMENT EXPERIENCE AND TURN IT INTO A BILLION-DOLLAR GLOBAL FRANCHISE LIKE COCA-COLA OR NIKE.

WITH VINCE JUNIOR... WELL, BEFORE YOU SIGNED ANYTHING HE GAVE YOU, IT WAS A GOOD IDEA TO RUN IT PAST TEN LAWYERS FIRST (BERNIE SPIEGEL).

VINCE McMAHON

AND IF YOU'RE WONDERING HOW JUNIOR COULD TAKE A REGIONAL PRO WRESTLING COMPANY AND TURN IT INTO THE LARGEST SPORTS ENTERTAINMENT COMPANY IN THE WORLD IN A MATTER OF YEARS, I'LL EXPLAIN...

I'LL SAY THIS NOW, I DIDN'T CARE FOR JUNIOR AS MUCH AS I HAD FOR SENIOR. THE OLDER VINCE WAS A MAN OF HIS WORD. IN ALL THE TIME I WORKED FOR SENIOR, I'D NEVER HAD TO SIGN A CONTRACT; OUR HANDSHAKE AGREEMENT WAS ENOUGH.

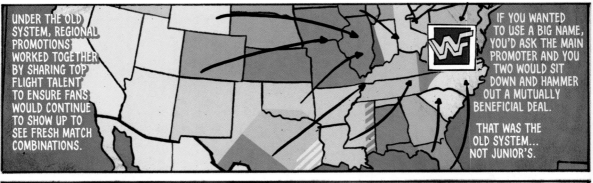

UNDER THE OLD SYSTEM, REGIONAL PROMOTIONS WORKED TOGETHER BY SHARING TOP FLIGHT TALENT TO ENSURE FANS WOULD CONTINUE TO SHOW UP TO SEE FRESH MATCH COMBINATIONS.

IF YOU WANTED TO USE A BIG NAME, YOU'D ASK THE MAIN PROMOTER AND YOU TWO WOULD SIT DOWN AND HAMMER OUT A MUTUALLY BENEFICIAL DEAL.

THAT WAS THE OLD SYSTEM... NOT JUNIOR'S.

JUNIOR BROKE THE CODE... HE POACHED GUYS FROM ALL OVER...

FROM THE MID-ATLANTIC REGION HE GRABBED RICKY STEAMBOAT, RODDY PIPER, GREG VALENTINE, BOB ORTON...

FROM BILL WATTS' MID-SOUTH PROMOTION HE GRABBED THE JUNKYARD DOG...

JUNIOR MERCILESSLY GUTTED VERNE GAGNE'S AWA PROMOTION SO THOROUGHLY THAT THEY NEVER TRULY RECOVERED FROM THE LOSS OF THESE IRREPLACEABLE TALENTS.

IN ONE FELL SWOOP, JUNIOR MANAGED TO BUILD A ROSTER OF LEGENDS WHILE SIGNIFICANTLY WEAKENING A FEW OF HIS TERRITORIAL RIVALS.

IN HOGAN, JUNIOR GOT THE ALL-AMERICAN SUPERHERO THAT HE NEEDED TO BE THE PUBLIC FACE OF HIS COMPANY.

I REALIZED THAT WHILE I WAS STILL AN "ATTRACTION" I WAS NO LONGER "THE MAN." IT WAS HOGAN'S TURN TO RUN WITH THE BALL. HE WAS MORE THAN CAPABLE. ALL THAT REMAINED WAS FINDING A VEHICLE TO GET HIS PRODUCT TO THE MASSES.

WF WRESTLEMANIA

I CALL IT... WRESTLEMANIA!

MARCH 31 1985

MADISON SQUARE GARDEN

THIS WAS THE ULTIMATE GAMBLE FOR JUNIOR. IF HIS "WRESTLEMANIA" THING FELL FLAT, THE COMPANY MIGHT NOT BE ABLE TO RECOUP THEIR LOSSES.

I'LL SAY THIS FOR VINCE JR., HE CERTAINLY KNEW HOW TO PULL OUT ALL THE STOPS IN THE QUEST FOR SUCCESS.

LIBERACE WAS THE GUEST TIMEKEEPER AND DANCED WITH THE ROCKETTES IN THE MIDDLE OF THE RING. NEVER IN MY WILDEST DREAMS DID I THINK I'D SEE SOMETHING LIKE THAT AT A WRESTLING SHOW!

I WAS INVOLVED IN A BODY SLAM CHALLENGE AGAINST MY LATEST ENEMY: BIG JOHN STUDD, MANAGED BY BOBBY "THE BRAIN" HEENAN. THE STIPULATION WAS SIMPLE, WHOMEVER SLAMMED THEIR OPPONENT FIRST WALKED OUT WITH $15,000!

I SLAMMED STUDD AND DECIDED TO TOSS THE CASH OUT TO THE CROWD. MUCH TO THE CHAGRIN OF HEENAN.

THE MAIN EVENT WAS EPIC... HOGAN AND HOLLYWOOD SUPERSTAR MR. T. VS. RODDY PIPER AND "MR. WONDERFUL" PAUL ORNDORFF.

THE PEOPLE LOVED WRESTLEMANIA. THE WWF BECAME A TRUE ENTERTAINMENT OPTION FOR MILLIONS OF VIEWERS ACROSS THE WORLD.

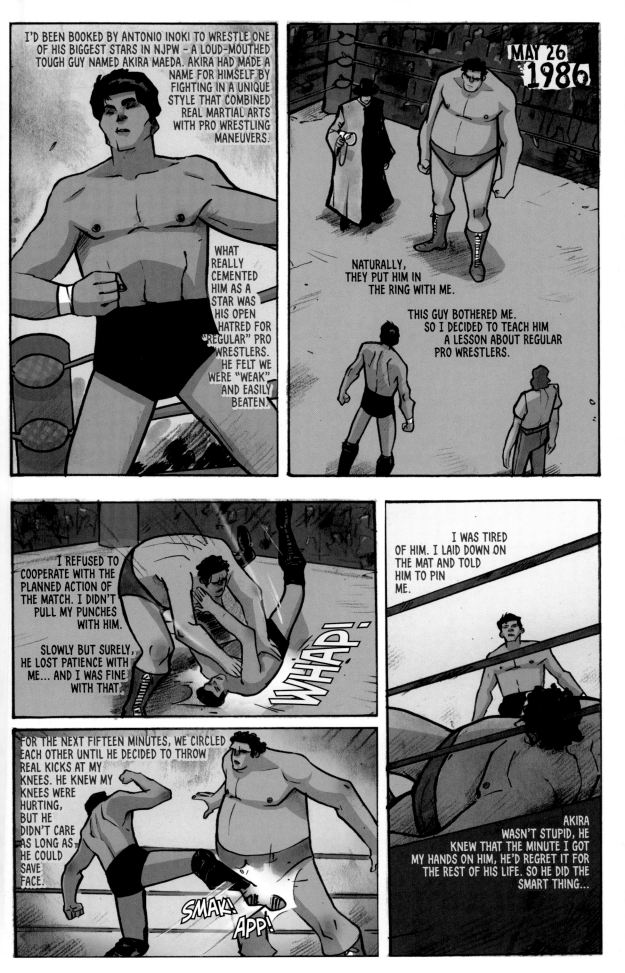

...HE GOT THE HELL OUT OF THERE.

THERE WERE DAYS WHEN I HATED OPENING MY EYES... ALL I HAD TO LOOK FORWARD TO WERE TWELVE HOURS OF TORTURE.

AND SOMETIMES THE LAUGHTER OF A CHILD COULD MAKE IT ALL DISAPPEAR.

VINCE JUNIOR HAD A DAUGHTER NAMED STEPHANIE.

I CALLED HER MY "LITTLE ANGEL" AND I THINK I SUBSTITUTED STEPHANIE FOR MY LOST RELATIONSHIP WITH ROBIN.

HOW'S MY LITTLE ANGEL?

GIGGLE

I FELL IN LOVE WITH THAT LITTLE GIRL, SHE NEVER ONCE SHOWED AN OUNCE OF FEAR WHEN WE FIRST MET.

THERE WERE GROWN MEN WHO COULDN'T MAKE THAT CLAIM.

THEY WANT ME TO PLAY A GIANT? I THINK I CAN DO THAT. WHAT'S THE NAME-?

"THE PRINCESS BRIDE?" HEH!

THEN I GOT A CALL ABOUT APPEARING IN A FAIRY TALE MOVIE. IT PIQUED MY INTEREST.

AFTER THE PRODUCTION WRAPPED, I COULDN'T TAKE THE PAIN ANYMORE. I REACHED OUT TO THE BEST BACK PHYSICIANS IN THE WORLD AND WAS SENT TO LONDON'S CROMWELL HOSPITAL. THEY NEEDED TO CUT MY BACK OPEN AND WIDEN MY SPINE OR ELSE I WOULDN'T BE ABLE TO WALK, LET ALONE WRESTLE EVER AGAIN.

I HAD TO WAIT ABOUT NINETY DAYS BEFORE THEY COULD OPERATE.

THEY NEEDED TO CONSTRUCT A LARGER BED, BIGGER SURGICAL TOOLS AND THEY EVEN BROUGHT A SMALL CRANE JUST IN CASE THEY HAD TO MOVE ME DURING THE DELICATE PROCEDURE.

MR. ROUSSIMOFF... WHAT ELSE WOULD YOU LIKE?

BEER.

THE SURGERY WAS A SUCCESS, BUT I WOULD NEED A WHILE TO FULLY RECUPERATE. IN THE MEANTIME, I GOT TO SEE MY FAMILY MEMBERS, INCLUDING MY NIECES AND NEPHEWS. SUDDENLY, MY WORLD DIDN'T FEEL SO EMPTY.

WE'VE ALREADY BROKEN MULTIPLE HEALTH CODES TO BRING YOU ALCOHOL, NOW TELL ME WHAT ELSE WOULD MAKE YOU COMFORTABLE?

BEER.

SERIOUSLY?

MORE BEER.

NOW I'M COMFORTABLE.

VINCE'S PLAN WAS BRILLIANT. I'D NEVER BEEN THE "BAD GUY" IN THE UNITED STATES SO THE BIG TURN WOULD SHOCK FANS, PARTICULARLY THE LITTLE KIDS THAT LOOKED UP TO ME.

WRESTLEMAN III

SO HE CONCOCTED AN ANGLE FOR ME TO CHALLENGE HOGAN... WHILE MAKING THE FANS HATE ME.

I'D APPROACHED HOGAN ON THE PIPER'S PIT SEGMENT OF THE WWF TV SHOW... WITH HOGAN'S ETERNAL NEMESIS BOBBY "THE BRAIN" HEENAN. YOU COULD HEAR THE FANS MURMUR IN CONFUSION ALONGSIDE HOGAN.

THEN I SAID HE DIDN'T RESPECT ME ENOUGH TO GIVE ME A TITLE SHOT EVEN THOUGH I'D BEEN "UNDEFEATED" MY ENTIRE CAREER. I DEMANDED A SHOT THEN AND THERE.

AND TO SHOW HOW SERIOUS I WAS, I RIPPED HIS "HULKAMANIA" SHIRT OFF HIS CHEST, UNKNOWINGLY DRAWING BLOOD WHEN HIS CRUCIFIX CUT INTO HIS SKIN.

IT WAS MARVELOUS.

AND DULL THE PAIN.

I SPENT MORE AND MORE TIME AT MY RANCH IN ELLERBE, NORTH CAROLINA.

I HAD A SPECIAL CHAIR BUILT FOR ME BECAUSE MY FAVORITE ACTIVITY HAD BECOME SITTING.

I COULD FEEL THE DARKNESS CREEPING IN FROM THE SIDES, LIKE HOW WATER SNEAKS INTO GOGGLES IN A DEEP SWIMMING POOL.

THERE WAS A PART OF ME THAT WAS AFRAID. NO MATTER HOW MUCH PAIN I WAS IN, I DIDN'T WANT TO DIE.

I'D DONE SO MUCH, AND FELT THAT THERE WAS SO MUCH MORE TO SEE AND EXPERIENCE.

JANUARY 1993

I WAS AFRAID THAT MY SINS FAR OUTWEIGHED MY GOOD DEEDS. I WONDERED IF ROTTEN KHARMA WAS WAITING FOR ME ON THE OTHER SIDE.

WHEN I PICKED UP THE PHONE, I LEARNED THAT MY FATHER BORIS DIDN'T HAVE MUCH TIME LEFT. I NEEDED TO GET TO FRANCE BEFORE IT WAS TOO LATE.

RRRRRRRRRNNNNNGGGGG

ANDRE "THE GIANT" ROUSSIMOFF

PASSED AWAY ON JANUARY 27TH, 1993. HE LEFT BEHIND A DAUGHTER, ROBIN CHRISTENSEN ROUSSIMOFF AND A LEGION OF CLOSE FRIENDS, COLLEAGUES, AND FANS ALL OVER THE EARTH.

ANDRE WAS CREMATED AND HIS ASHES SPREAD OVER HIS FARM IN ELLERBE, NORTH CAROLINA. ANDRE'S FARM WAS TENDED BY HIS CONFIDANT FRENCHY BERNARD UNTIL HIS OWN DEATH IN SEPTEMBER, 2013.

ANDRE THE GIANT CHANGED THE SPORT OF PRO WRESTLING FOREVER AND WAS THERE AT EVERY MOMENT OF ITS EXPANSION INTO A GLOBAL ENTITY.

ANDRE TOUCHED THE LIVES OF MILLIONS AND EVEN TWO DECADES AFTER HIS PASSING, HIS NAME ECHOES ON IN THE HEARTS AND MINDS OF TRUE WRESTLING FANS EVERYWHERE.

IF HE WERE HERE TODAY, AND COULD SEE HOW MANY PEOPLE STILL LOVE AND MISS HIM, HE'D PROBABLY SAY HIS FAVORITE PHRASE:

"THANKS, BOSS..."

FIN.

THE
SIX MILLION
DOLLAR MAN

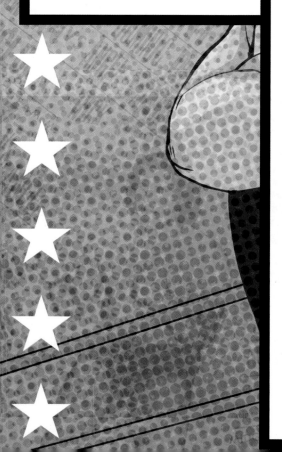

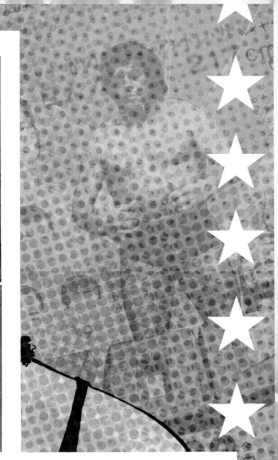

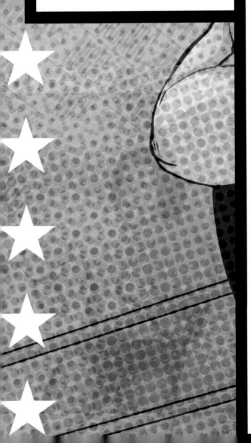